r e v e r b e r a t i o n s

SUNY Series, Feminist Philosophy
Jeffner Allen, Editor

r e v e r b e r a t i o n s

across the shimmering   CASCADAS

JEFFNER ALLEN

STATE UNIVERSITY OF NEW YORK PRESS

"On the Seashore, A Writing of Abundance" appears in an earlier version in *Lesbian Philosophies and Cultures*, ed. Jeffner Allen (Albany: SUNY Press, 1991).

"Passion in the Gardens of Delight" appears in earlier versions in *Women of Power* 13 and *An Intimate Wilderness: Lesbian Writers on Sexuality*, ed. Judith Barrington (Portland: The Eighth Mountain Press, 1991).

Published by State University of New York Press, Albany
© 1994 Jeffner Allen

For information, address State University of New York Press,
State University Plaza, Albany, N.Y., 12246

Production by Marilyn P. Semerad
Marketing by Theresa A. Swierzowski

Library of Congress Cataloging-in-Publication Data

Allen, Jeffner, 1947-
    Reverberations : across the shimmering CASCADAS / Jeffner Allen.
       p.   cm. — (SUNY series, feminist philosophy)
    ISBN 0-7914-1897-9 (acid-free paper). — ISBN 0-7914-1898-7 (pbk.
: acid-free paper)
    1. Lesbianism—Philosophy—Poetry. 2. Feminism—Philosophy-
-Poetry. I. Title. II. Series.
PS3551.L39382R48 1994
811'.54—dc20   93-31711
                                                                   CIP

10 9 8 7 6 5 4 3 2 1

Contents

invitations

These abundance writings are intimate chattings that celebrate collisions   transitions unexpected   that welcome fluidity   a breathing   that traverse deaths and lives   what you i we and we may scarcely bear to remember or to say   too easy or too hard or too painful   events that cannot be rushed through   *How to love where there may be nothing in common or this today and (not) that tomorrow?* The spacious writing of these *r e v e r b e r a t i o n s* gathers and dissolves   *with nearby* joy sorrow grief compassion   *alongside   on the edges of* womyn loving womyn longings womyn lovings and womyn storms   *across* genocides murders crashes economic depriva- tions nationalisms ___   and out of this   SEVERALS SUR- PRISING   a healing   perhaps

and she turned the gourd   flower on top flower on the bottom   in her hands   words carved into its surface   you and she turned the gourds round and around and read   but from where you she i i and i read   upwards downwards or in which directions   i could not tell   a sad story   a war   destroyed lives   you said   and now after the war   separations deaths reunions and . . .   yet whether she who would come alive   all that would come alive over and over   she or we or you   were looking at the gourds at all   stories flying into bodies   into other stories   perched   metal piercing flesh   in the retelling   glass   overhead three jump   ropes a flying snake flying   you she i turned the gourds round and around flowers on the tops   flowers green caterpillars on the bottoms   and tonight

the gourds fly off   kites in strong winds cannot be held by
strings and kites where there is no wind may fall into the sea
while they and we and we tell stories

   or kites may float up   *found pieces*
   if you are squeamish don't prod the beach rubble   which
washes up when what will not assimilate has been expelled
   on the shore   amid rubble washed by the sea   you gather a
handful of shells   i pick up a shell seaweed stones
   between among whatever comes to through past around
you you i i you i   *countless passages*   complex worlds   gra-
tuitous parts   autobiography   poetry   feminist theory   les-
bian studies   multicultural writing   postmodernism   theo-
ries of writing   womyn loving womyn   *not to discard*
persistent disturbances   to resist continuous prunings that
would mark the random as not functional and breed it out

   spaces to wander   to bypass   to skip on through
                              this is not a travelogue   ?

Landscapes passed through but not devastated   loving
befriending surviving in difficult times without dominating
   i have always wanted to write a travelogue / this is not a
travelogue   where travel may be a birthing *travail* / the hard
   work of birthing   also *travail* / where travel may be an
instrument of torture having three or more stakes *tripalium*
at a time when travel agents   for a price   would supply the
itinerary   tickets for the journey accommodations without
discomfort   travel guides
   In intimacy how to cultivate wilderness?

   these slow unfoldings of hearts   estos despliegues lentos de cora-
zones   espaciostiempos miriadas entre   que vuelan y se
   chocan   en los cuales nosotras nosotras tu yo ni nos
quedamos ni partimos incambiadas   myriad spacestimes
between   that fly and collide   in which we we you i neither
   stay nor leave unchanged   the arrangement of the writ-

ings in this book is chronological   is to be found at any moment
    '*On the Seashore,* A Writing of Abundance'   clitoral cur-
    rents   writings not instrumental   'Passion in the Gardens
of Delight'   blue butterfly   ethics slips into aesthetics   ecolo-
gies of the emotions   these slow unfoldings   to read to one-
self   read aloud   listen to   sing   sights and sounds each
time not the same
    Sonic writings   surprises confusions   to improvise
'S P I R I T S'   genocide   racism   sally bell   the lost coast
    ancestors   jumping rope   in one of the most populated
native regions of north america   '*r e v e r b e r a t i o n s*
    moonflowers   estrellas fugaces   *r e v e r b e r a c i o n e s*
    flores lunares   falling stars'   dos semanas o tiempos
indefinidos   two weeks or indefinite times   maritza   sandía
maría luisa   new york   buenos aires   río   mercedes   maría
northern california   las hermanas de la mar   your sisters of
the sea   and the language?   english / english spanish /
spanish spanish / english english / spanish   lengua casi
familiar y no muy familiar   *i understand you   but   language
almost familiar and not quite familiar*   te entiendo   pero   not
to carry across by force   to resist a forced crossing   resistir
una travesía forzada   no llevar al través a la fuerza   y donde
    hay travesías *irregulares   no-secuenciales   no-intercambiables*
quizás hay solamente travesías   and where there are cross-
ings   *irregular non-sequential   non-interchangeable*   perhaps
there are only crossings   mouths unstable   forgetful wan-
dering   liable to slip   mouths slipping across deaths lives
arms   hands   yemas de dedo   legs   climbing up   *brazos
manos   fingertips   piernas*   subiendo arriba   connective tis-
sues muscles webbing   cuentame como estás   cuentame
    algo de tí   besitos y un abrazo   *tell me how you are*   tell
me something about yourself   kisses a hug   and   'tea on
the beach at midnight'

a page of mouths a book of mouths
    where what is heard and what is seen are several   where

no longer is I with bars at head and feet   bars   cages of the
WE   iii yiyouyiouyou break free   do   do not   recognize
ourselves each other   have never really been together *in* I
WE
   a nebular i of shifting densities darknesses florescence
  now i live multiples of you wandering you divining   til
you i vanish   i   you   i you you i i   i i you i   *pinksunburned*
whitei walking   you i shifting not isolate   sounds in motion
tu tu yo nosotras y nosotras   you you i we and we   hemisfe-
rios   distinct and not entirely distinct   hemispheres   distin-
tos y no enteramente distintos   this jef-u.s.a.-i   this jef-u.s.a.-
you   configuraciones conflictivas   ésas   ésa jef-ee.uu.-yo
ésa jef-ee.uu.-tu   conflicted configurations   these   *& una*
frisbee mandarina   & a tangerine frisbee   her she you i
invoked by wayside markers that obscure   intervals neither
fused nor entirely distinct

las CASCADAS

silenciosreverberantessonidosreverberantes
reverberentsilencesreverberentsounds
   for eyes in the ears that wind and unwind down bodies
between bodies down and around bodies to the feet
   difference tones   *you i have been   are still resounding*
with tones which have been   are still   resounding   and you i may
  may not have heard any of these tones   marejadas de sonido
soundswells   to let vibrate until the sounds and silences fade
away   dejar vibrar hasta que los sonidos y silencios se
  apaguen   y que se abren ruidosamente   and that open
noisily   a sea of microtones   ambiguous tones of differ-
ing intervals and unexpected effects   that color the hearts of
you I she her   sonic shadows   echoes in a valley as unfin-
ished conversations touch

   a writing discovers herself with others
  ii you i thank many friends   and melyssa jo kelly   jeanne
constable   nicole brossard   celeste baross   maría lugones

van allen   pauline oliveros   sarah hoagland   lauren crux
sarah douglas   gloria anzaldúa   anne mamary   faye new-
field   kim hall   kate miller   bettina aptheker   joyce trebilcot
    and lois patton at SUNY Press   i am grateful to Cottages at
Hedgebrook for an invitation to be a writer in residence
spring 1991

*fragantes con mimosa   wisteria   fragrant with   mimosa   vistaria
jazmines   bouganvilla*   UNSTABLE JUNCTIONS   ESLA-
BONES DISYUNTIVOS
    no one point   nevertheless crossings departures and
arrivals   where *each moment each movement* minutely affects
moments movements   languages and memories   each i
you we   grating strained   lenguas y memorias   *cada yo tu
nosotras* asperá torcida   *caminando en el agua saltanto de
piedra en piedra   buscando un sentido para cruzar   wading rock-
hopping looking for a way to cross*   puentes flotantes   floating
bridges   unstable junctions of midnight and morning

celebrations   you she i turn the gourds round and around
    you sail to islands luminous in the mist and silver dawn
i sail to islands pink at sunset and sunrise   *have you lived a
great love?   ¿has vivido un gran amor?*   the space between is
not empty to be feared but waves in which you i swim and
sometimes embrace   how to say your sorrow is my sorrow
    your happiness is my happiness?   *how do i i lunar rose you
i she love?*

On the Seashore,
A Writing of Abundance

The economy of scarcity that I live daily makes difficult and vital the conception of a writing of abundance. Writing, when reduced by the economy of scarcity to an instrument in the service of something other than itself—even when used as a means for 'revolution', or a tool for the acquisition of 'knowledge'—vanishes from thought.

Yet the wonder I find is that the powers of writing defy eclipse: are not the physical, emotional, and intellectual famines of life under patriarchy ended, in part, when writing, remembered, brings forth a writing of abundance?

There was a time before there was a war, before abundance was rendered scarce and the many were dominated by the Same.

I am drawn to this time, to the shores of a writing which *is* an abundance. Abundance, flowing with the waves and without bounds, is an inexhaustible plentitude.

In a field of wildflowers where never has there been any question but that each is herself, gentle Gaiety, Revelry, Radiance, and Muses with lovely hair offer a welcoming embrace. 'Woman', the word which has betokened the constriction of female existence as womb and wife of man, dissolves in myriad currents: womon, womyn, wimmin.

A time before there was a war, a time of abundance, is an invention. An invention is not plucked out of the air and imposed on reality as if that were a blank slate awaiting definition. Invention approaches that which is there. When I invent a time I come to a time which already comes to me.

I set down my pen, I close this book and writing does not stop. I open this book, I pick up my pen, and writing does not begin. The writing is not a gimmick I manipulate by whim, but an event with its own histories.

Writing is the greeting in which a writing births herself. Writing is the welcoming of that freedom.

Writing is not the mark that would impress itself on random points in empty space. Nor is writing the frame that would captivate language by its pre-formed focus, stasis. The institution of a center, the confinement to the Same, miss the freedom of writing.

Writing *is* in the open rapport of the many. Writings of the past, star writings of the future, traverse again and again the plants, earth, self, with which they are inscribed.

A writing is in company with, and not imposed on, parchment, clay tablet, consciousness. A writing is ancient and contemporary, she discovers herself with others.

The coming to be of a writing as she *is* is a conception by parthenogynesis.

Goddesses are born of writing; goddesses each of whom brings forth a writing. The ancient wisdom of H.D., "blue as the blue-poppy, / blue as the flax in flower," she who knows our fears, remembers, and who does not falter, the meditative knowledge of Elsa Gidlow, a "knowledge standing stark under the sky / feet naked to earth," is each a goddess of writing free from the disguise of authority, bold, and beautiful.

The shore is effervescent: shifting sands, rubble washed by the sea, layers under layers upon layers. There is a transformation of energies in these multiple, shifting, grounds.

Among the tens of thousands of languages, the language I speak is a language situated in writing. Where writing is, worlds in writing and the being of worlds are inseparable.

I emerge with this writing, a nebular I.

The I of authority, disciplinary I that would judge writing from a distance, transparent I for whom writing must be to become legible for everyone even if indecipherable for oneself, loses hold before an I of shifting densities, darknesses, florescence.

Clitoral currents trace shimmering galaxies of visceral desire.

The effulgences of lesbian love and writing celebrate the intensities of mutual delight. It is a matter of significance that clitoral currents are lesbian: warm, billowing, radiant.

Sensual and scriptural configurations are at play when writing is cyprine.*

Alphabets of wimmin, the many alphabets of each woman, survive: the clay tablets and cuneiform of Nidaba of Sumer,

---

*A secretion of lesbian lovers [from *Cyprus*, birthplace of Aphrodite].

the letters of the three Fates, parthenogynic daughters of the Great Goddess, and of Io, the violet flower, moon that encircles the Mediterranean. How could I have thought the syllables of Sarasvati, signs of Kali, hieroglyphs of Isis, whom Serpot of Syria, Amazon queen, invoked as goddess of the land of womyn, woman's contribution to *the* alphabet?

Alphabets, delightful surfaces, magical signs, cosmic vibrations intertwine, making writing festive.

On the shore, amid rubble washed by the sea, I live. My memory is a beginning, not first, but as always, opening to times spaces Myceneas future and past.

My memory travels with a writing before which the dissolution of patriarchy is a matter of fact.

The dead live when the moist lotus open along Acheron.

Lost continents of writing are sites from which I see the horrors and undergo healing.

I forget the claim to reality that is made by the Same when, aware that claim is being made, I move apart from its hold.

Lovers of writing turn the leaves of memories and books, tending, patching, mending.

The mysteries of writing are not a secret to be withheld, but an experience that is brimming with life.

Yet where is the writing when our books are so few, and when so many are banned, lost?

Writing, too, travels with memory. By this power writing preserves herself when memory endures the flames in which a writing is burned. On byways such as these Sappho's lyric poetry survives the destructions of Alexandria by Christians and Moslems.

But at times, a writing is burned, and the more that is written the more quickly it is burned, or suppressed . . . out of date, incomplete, unreal, disquieting. If you are squeamish don't prod the beach rubble, which washes up when what will not assimilate is expelled.

No longer the captivity of writing!

On indigenous grounds a writing thrives. Her powers cannot be made to grow on alien terrain.

With a magic eye, tooth, and Gorgon face, the three Fates find at each season a writing: twigs scattered by the wind, drifting sands, the flight of birds.

But if this writing in her freedom were to meet the limit once, and once again, the eye of mastery that would seize her in its grasp, the sickle that would cut her off from perception, divination, rebirth, the craneskin bag that would contain her, the mask that would frighten away her friends, if she were to encounter Hermes, hermeneut who thinks stones are mute, he who would bring her from unintelligibility to intelligibility—according to whom?—she might forget life, were not she tenacious.

The lie: that Hermes has the alphabet. That by cunning theft Hermes stole writing from the three Fates. That he was given the gift of writing by the three Fates. That he is the origin of writing and language.

Writing is not one and writing cannot be possessed. The three Fates did not give writing to Hermes, nor did Agluaros give Hermes her daughter, Herse, moon goddess of the morning dew.

I remember the attempts made by force, over time, to break the power of memory; to instill the belief that writing must be captive.

I remember the teaching that writing is a writing of servitude, porno-graphy, a writing that affirms its submission to the Same, that writing must comply when the chain of command of a grammar where the subject governs verb and thereby possesses object comes to power. I remember the attempts to inculcate the lesson that I, if I am to write, must also be captive.

Hermes, communications technology satellite, circles the earth, while wild mares frolic on the shore.

The attempt to use writing counting cattle and counting wimmin, counting what cannot be counted, is at the origins of scarcity and civilization.

Civilization would turn writing against herself.

The history of writing in the West, as set forth in vase painting, 600 b.c.—300 a.d., in mainland Greece, the Black sea, Anatolia, and Europe, depicts a history in which men, but never wimmin, write. That history attests to the fact that wimmin who write, and all wimmin caring for pleasure and freedom, live in ways that escape representation by civilization.

A writing of six hundred ideographs circulates solely among womyn in Jiangyong County, Hunan province, 960 a.d. to the present. The womyn, barred from school and confined to the home, write. While weaving, the womyn read the writing to each other.

Young womyn form families of sworn sisters and write of these sisterhoods in womyn characters. They continue to communicate in the writing after marriage. They burn their writings so that in the next life they can enjoy them. The womyn believe that the script came to Hu Xiuying during her loneliness at the imperial palace.

Wimmin often have no option between non-literacy and literacy: sixty-two percent of the non-literate people in the world are wimmin, the gap between the percentage of wimmin and men who are non-literate is increasing.

Wimmin who are literate often are obliged to a literacy that would confirm the legitimacy of civilization.

In memory

Two womyn teachers in Afghanistan, 1984, are raped, mutilated, and burned on a fire of school books. The womyn taught reading and writing and did not wear veils.

Over five thousand years ago, in Sumer, a region of southern Babylonia, Nidaba appears with clay tablets and cuneiform, prior to any of the male gods who attempt to replace her. Yet by 1880-1550 b.c., wimmin in Sippar, a city in northern Babylonia, write in the *gagûm*: a locked house inside the walled temple dedicated to the sun god, Sāmaš. The wimmin who write are *nadītu*, the barren ones: without children and without property.

Iltani, who composes her last text when she is more than seventy, Inaan-amamu, Amat-Mamu, a scribe for at least forty years, and Awāt-Aja, are among the *nadītu* who write the lives of the one hundred to two hundred wimmin who reside, at the same time, in the locked house.

The *nadītu* often live to be old, for they do not die in childbirth, which shortened the lives of many womyn. They offer each other mutual support. Within the confines of the locked house, they enjoy a degree of personal freedom exceptional for womyn at that time.

At birth the womyn are marked, given names to show they are destined for the locked house. They are sent to the *gagûm* so that, upon their death, their share of the paternal estate will be inherited by their brothers. Under an administrative staff comprised exclusively of men, the *nadītu* keep records of sales and profits from the land.

At the center of the city womyn write, provided that womyn and writing are walled in.

Cloaked, wimmin with writing walk in the heart of the city. Axiothea, in the fourth century b.c., leaves home and travels to Athens where, disguised as a man, she becomes a student. Hypatia, 375-415 a.d., casts a cloak around herself and appears in Alexandria, where she teaches and writes mathematics, astronomy, philosophy, and mechanics. Hypatia is killed when men tear off her cloak and mutilate her body because she is a womon, because she will not convert to Christianity, because she will not leave the city with her teaching and writing.

Wimmin with writing walk in the city by assuming the appearance of men, and at the will of men.

Why do I write?

I leave the blue springs and blazing sun, the tropics, pink azaleas and palms, to live in the city with a lesbian writing. At my job, I circulate among languages, none of them my own, and when I write I am told, "not philosophy," "poetry," ". . . using language as it was not intended."

I partake in migrations not sought, but taken on, to be to myself a writing companion and for economic sustenance, to make real a world that enlivens my senses, to be with friends. I live with the excitement of beauty in the open, a writing of cultures of womyn on the lost coast, llamas, red humming-birds, wild berries, sea gulls, when I am told, "not the ideal woman we had in our minds."

And now, on the frontier, a bare winter after years of sea and sun, why is this winter so cold?

Is it possible to write without moon, sun, stars, the warmth of wimmin?

The mysteries

The war is over what is not. Writing is not possessed by Hermes, womyn are not in civilization, counting counts only its own numbers, marks only its bills of ownership and sales, the limit limits itself.

I write over, under, across the limit, apart from the limit, without the limit.

In psychic gathering I find a writing that lives with the cosmic. I meet with a time that flows.

Through magic greater than the force of Hermes, a time before there was a war becomes also a time that is now.

Silver streaks from waves to shore, a writing, buoyant, arrives with a gasp. She brings with her gentle breezes, a cosmic shedding. A writing that may exceed language, she brings feeling, touch, free movement.

On the seashore boats at sunset and sunrise bring local crops, quilts, seashells, scrolls. Lavender ribbons, currency from a time when wimmin recorded ownership and debt, pile up in disuse. Nets shine with new values.

Wimin glean curiously shaped alphabets from events on boat and shore, telling the stories, pain, anger, and joys, which are and can be in the present of our lives.

A writing discovers herself with others

SAPPHO   H.D.   ELSA GIDLOW   SAPPHO   H.D.   ELSA
GIDLOW   SAPPHO   H.D.   H.D.   NICOLE BROSSARD
MONIQUE WITTIG   H.D.   MICHELLE CAUSSE   SAPPHO

Susan
Guettel
Cole,
"Could
Greek
Women
Read and
Write?"
*Reflections
of Women
in
Antiquity*,
edited
by Helen
P. Foley,
1981

"Secret
Women's
Writing,"
Audrey
Mindlin,
SpareRib
1986

"500
Million
Illiterate
Women
Worldwide:
Female/Male
Gap
Increases,"
WIN News
13.1:36

The Status of
Women in
Afghanistan,"
WIN News
12.4:48

Margaret
Alic,
*Hypatia's
Heritage*,
1986

Rivkah
Harris,
"Biographical
Notes on the
Naditu
Women of
Sippar,"
*Journal of
Cuneiform
Studies* 16
(1962): 1-12

Ulla Jeyes,
"The Naditu
Women of
Sippar,"
*Images of
Women in
Antiquity*,
edited by
Averil Cameron
and Amelie
Kuhrt, 1983

SAPPHO   H.D.   BRYHER   MICHELLE CAUSSE
ELSA GIDLOW   NICOLE BROSSARD   MONIQUE WITTIG
SAPPHO   H.D.   H.D.   SAPPHO

Passion in the Gardens of Delight

Blue butterfly morning glory heart no longer dead of heart now I live multiples of you wandering you divining. Blue butterfly morning glory heart no longer dead of heart leapfrog somersault until you I vanish.

Flying breathing we touch the roundness of being.

Butterflies light on my hair when books are closed and I forget my lessons. Then you I race to the rivers of life and we dive in.

The dance of the marvelous and the believable   jumping jumping jumping still bouncing bouncing jumping jumping you I desiring melting meadows forest clouds jumping you I breezes sun jumping still looking desiring melting feet leave ground ground feet smiling smiling twinkling dissolving twinkling melting meadows forest clouds sun lift whirl turbulence freeflow twinkling is there a touch overturns everything jumping jumping surprisingly surprised.

By the sunflowers you I pick the petals. She loves me.

Two eyes looking at two eyes two hands holding two hands hold eyes in palms eyes bring to see alchemical equations life lines of earth blood red of fire ocean.

The intensity of living things awakens us when skin to skin on a clear night you I glide with the stars and moon feeling how what might be is.

The most perfect of spiderwebs may catch a butterfly fly-
ing into another dimension. The web breaks. The butterfly flies
on.

Moving through time is sorcery magic simple anticipation. Horizons turn cartwheels the present whirls by you I skip along.

You sail to islands luminous in the mist and silver dawn. I sail to islands pink at sunset and sunrise. The space between is not empty to be feared but waves in which you I swim and sometimes embrace.

Delight runs free delights in running free

The North 40 *Lavender Jane Loves Wimmin* a pond wimmin
sunning dipping lesbian concentrate ripples of excitement
energy mid-afternoon drifts away from the continent.

The delights of touch and tongue abound when paradise is lost. Delight is not found in paradise: *pairidaēza* an old Persian word from which the Hebrew and Greek terms are derived a walled garden the hunting park of the king. Delight is celebrated and written apart from hedges fences fortresses which would discipline freedom.

A small tree shrine to she of the wild appears between two arms of one stream flowing in opposite directions. The shrine at Ephesus is on marshy grounds to move with the earth when the earth shakes.

Dancing a round dance a shield dance quivers rattling amazons are with hawks ibex bulls axes sphinx wings rising tail arched boar mane rising eye in the shape of a flower petal horse rising from the waves. A winged goddess grasps two lions at the root of their tails and holds the lions downward forepaws touching the ground heads turned upward with open jaws snarling.

The marsh is drained by king Croesus in the sixth century b.c. The Artemision monumental edifice one of the wonders of the world is erected over tree shrine hawks double-axes amazons.

A morning glory winds along disappears reappears sometimes takes life on the way and blossoms each morning.

Sky rock water you I leap from ledge to ledge around the fire that brightens cliffs night skies. At dawn you I slip into the sea.

NO NUDISM NO CAMPING read orange plastic signs in French German English Greek posted on Lesbos by Sun Med Holidays. At Scala Eressos rugged hills red poppies blue water the beach is bulldozed by tractors. Wimmin no longer gather outsider and knit fishing boats no longer land on the shore olive trees are cut down property is bound by barbed wire.

When in the mist the land floats above the sea you I curl around each other at the end of the beach.

Composing   weeds   worms the connection of the elements
lets the earth grow   leaves the soil richer than it was before.

Ethics slips into aesthetics feeling flourishes without the command when slowly so slowly you I meet with ecologies of the emotions.

In intimacy how to cultivate wilderness? How to live in the wilds with the wilds emotions which escape the name? How to feel the futures which inhabit the blue glacial lakes?

Bare-skinned you I soar with the wind tumble to earth in the warm rain.

Not enough theory? The end of discipline? What if a field were to burst into bloom mountains become deserts washed by ocean?

Snap fingers cluck tongue   flutter   lips   touch   lips
flutter   tongues   harmonic   glissando   tambourine
rainbows   water   songs

We dance

If you have rushed to this point burn incense rest visit friends.

Clitoris tongue rolls over and over you I now alive vibrations all over clitoris tongue rolls over to kiss blue butterfly morning glory heart.

SPIRITS

blowing kisses to she who is not here   or is she?
what is a kiss   blowing kisses in the air?
          hello   good-bye
    or perhaps you are here already in   air   wind   sky

where do the kisses go?   dissolve   pop   like   bubbles?
    why blow kisses in the air
    why to she who is   is not   here
do they alight   do they take off   fly away?

kisses   tumbling   dancing   yellow   breezes
flowers   lips   feathers   on the beach
    a   huge   clear   blue   sky

is she here   is she the kiss
    your kisses her kissess my kissses a kiss's kissessss

    kisses when you arrive   kisses now   YES you are here
    and your kiss   pink yellow   is   exquisite

she i you   have lost track   are off the track   we celebrate
what else?

ARTEMIS: 'project control systems
for the Canadian and Northwest
Railway ...

suspension

breathing into each other   we sing

BLUE BLUE I LOVE YOU BEAUTIFUL
  BLUEILOVEYOU BEAUTIFUL   BLUE
I? YOU?   BLUE

skies below   skies above   three moons   cracks in the skies
stars glide   stars fly   stars run   stars slide   stars run away
morning stars   a rain of stars

laughing the stars return

not the same   and sometimes all at once   to improvise

surf seagulls wind   voices i hear   voices i do not hear
head on your breast   your breathing my breathing   her
i listen   you catch my attention   perhaps   sounds
silences   she simultaneous

the pacific ocean sounds not like the atlantic ocean sounds
not like the indian ocean sounds not like the mediterranean
sounds

hi   come on over   after all these years of you being the
   author?   what are you doing anyway?   *i'm not sure
i   can speak to you at you past you   but how do i hear you
   speak if i'm writing the page?*   why don't you move over?

                          TO AUTHOR: to manage voices well
                             to make sure voices have their
                            freedom and directly address
                                 their audience to say
                              there are merely relations
                                  between texts to
                                  rob each voice of
                                      her life

SHE SELLS SEA SHELLS BY THE SEA SHORE   who is
she!   first she thought she could write us off   now she
thinks she can write us up   but we're Not for sale   we're
Not for sale   Not even by her!

difference tones   two tones sounded simultaneously
produce a third tone which is equal to the difference in
frequency of the two tones sounded

difference tones   *you i have been   are still   resounding with*
tones which have been   are still   resounding   and you i may
may not have heard any of these tones

difference *tones   you i* shifting   not *isolate   are* who?
and how *many?   i lose* the count but not *the rhythm*
driftwood tones rolling through *hands   fingertips traced by*
vibrations of silence

neither sea serpents nor subways nor Sappho herself

the subject the object Iyou the mind the body   odorless
colorless seemingly white   receive a letter they do not quite
understand but decide to pursue   the 'necessary
distinctions' too long stored in the closet   assemble   take
off   are not heard of again   without sorrow

violets musk lavender sweat cut hay spring rain

no longer hanging descriptions on subjects   and unwilling
to play with assertions without considering matters of
freedom and power   the author went to the beach one day
and was UNDERMINED————without the author the
story becomes unclear————by a stormy swell   or some
say simply by entering the flowing waves

you she i came up on the shore

and with friends   you i ride the waves   dive under the
waves   while she rides a boogie board

sounds without signposts bring a leaping lesbian deadened by
proper pages of concepts back to life   slight wonder
Sappho wrote in a demi-lydian mode which like Sappho was
not from greece but from lydia or phygia   and more than
other modes was CHARGED WITH EMOTIONS

walking just to hear the waves

i saw the sun set today fire orange yellow sky pink all the
way around   i saw the sun rise today fire orange yellow
sky pink all the way around   back-bend cobra grasshopper
hands-to-feet crocodile wind boat

i   you   i you you i i   i i you i   circle turn circle circle fast
fast falling in the sand falling dizzy choreograph dizzily in
heaps

arms stretched out you turn fast faster   arms stretched
over head you fly   arms at sides i spin   slowly   hands
bump against hands   you you i sounds in motion collide
tumble at different speeds   and the spaces between i   you
i you you i i   i i you i   tumble collide spin on and on fly
the spaces between   the sites of collision   where there are i
you   i you you i i   i i you i

moon in the sky at midday   inattention to fluid motion and
to non-renewable resources brings acid rain   red red red red
         the color here is red

with among between i   you   i you you i i   i i you i   wave
marked sand   butterfly wings   a story   a herstory   a place
a dreaming   spirit paintings   have a thousand kinds ten
thousand ways

fingertips run along palms electric   eyes in palms not eyes that
scan the track   but eyes that travel into dream

on the lost coast   lost   too far west from highway ⬡**1** *where the*
ground does not rest   north american plate grinding over the pacific
plate   fracturing bedrock   unstable soil   *as the terrain lifts upward*
earth rising into sky   pelicans sea lions wild ginger blackberries
fairy bells lilies poppies oil slick exxon star flowers blue-eyed grass
periwinkles shooting stars   black sands smell of salt
pinksunburned whitei walk   *in one of the most populated native*
regions of north america   since 6000 b c e home of the sinkyone
indians

my grandfather and all of my family—my mother my
father and me—were around the house and not hurting
anyone   soon about ten o'clock in the morning   some
white men came   they killed my grandfather and my
mother and my father   i saw them do it   i was a big
girl at that time   then they killed my baby sister and
cut her heart out and threw it in the brush where i ran
and hid   my little sister was a baby just crawling
around   i didn't know what to do   i was so scared
that i guess i just hid there a long time   with my little
sister's heart in my hands   i felt so bad and i was so
scared that i just couldn't do anything else   then i ran
into the woods and hid there for a long time   i lived
there a long time with a few other people who had got
away

—sally bell

from "sinkyone notes" by gladys nomland   university of california publications in
american archaeology and ethnology vol 36 (2)   berkeley 1935   p 166

pinksunburned whitei walk for several days

in 1851 and 1852 california authorized over
one million dollars for white men to murder
native americans

trees of this grove are blood relatives who witnessed
native american history   to cut them down is murder
--dennis jennings

epic newsletter   (environmental protection information council)   march 9 1987
special issue on the sinkyone wilderness   with dennis jennings of the international
indian treaty council

while listening to the voices   i   you   i you you i i   i i you i
which travel in my direction   *pinksunburned whitei continue*
walking

abalone sea   outgoing tide   bluegreen clouds shimmer on
the sand   no waves edge the beach in the same ways   no
wave edges the beach in a straight line

echoes of the blood relatives as *pinksunburned whitei* splash
in the ocean with the birds   as *pinksunburned whitei* listen

no one point *red starfish* no precise *point sponges* sea snails no
fixed point anemones muscles no period *horseshoe crab* no point
seaweed *lightning glass* at which moons suns cross horizons
nevertheless   crossings departures and arrivals

these manifestations of severals   music texts of womyn loving
perhaps   SEVERALS SURPRISING   and out of severals
*wimmin loving wimmin longings wimmin lovings and wimmin
storms*   woman-identified   that you i are wimmin   but
among between with you i   commotion of sights herstories
sounds   SEVERALS SURPRISING which might   might not
might sometimes   in ways that elude identification   TOUCH

where what is heard and what is seen are several   where no
longer is I with bars at head and feet   bars to hold in place
bars locked interlocked with other bars   cages of the WE   to
assure that WE agree   bars flex bend as iiiyiyouyiouyou break
free   do   do not   recognize ourselves each other   have
never really been together *in* I WE

listening to   *telling*   *our lives*   *iiyouyouii*/⦚⦚⦚⦚ᵎᵎᵕ*ignite I*   *I WE*
ignites

music and texts in opposition transition   in question not in
propositions   to decline THE proposition   severals dancing
singing drumming in divergence convergence   interspersed
according to movements herstories emotions

a tree with no leaves   roots in air   rising from the sand
rooted in air sand and water?

and today   you you i tell emotions severals herstories severals
where each moment each movement minutely affects moments
movements

you tell of you you i who tell   gap indeterminate unknown
to this i   telling you she \\\   rift   the dangers still of
telling   *as you i listen for*

infrasounds   impact of ocean waves volcanoes earthquakes
blue whales elephants   ultrasounds   bats porpoises insects
shrews dykesounds   *when in looking you i at your my blood no
amount of fury is too much*   touched by earth water fire   your
lips coral reefs in desert sand   tropical reefs   petrified marine
animals that once populated the ocean   spiral windings of
shells polished by blasting of desert wind

cliffs   sand   water   sky   where you i walk with friends
listening telling touching   with a gentleness that undoes a tap a
blow

sandbuckets shovel i see her footprint in the sand   sandcastles
she says   wash out to sea with the tide   tomorrow   she says
she will make more castles   she continues scooping up
handfuls of wet sand   i gather feathers shells for sandcastles   i
ask her if i can join in

you and she   she says   on the lost coast wove ropes from the dried
leaves of the iris   played jump rope with an iris string by the trees
looking out at the ocean   jump rope tied to trees and held by friends
you she jumping jumping   i bring my favorite plastic with red
wood handles jump rope to the edges of her tale

i and she   she says   played jump rope with a green plastic rope by
the trees   looking out at the ocean   just before dinner time   jump
rope tied to trees and held by friends   i and she jumping jumping

a braid of dried iris leaves   a green plastic line   you i she
friends jump rope by *the trees of this grove looking listening out
over the ocean*   between these tales spaces of eight thousand
years or eighty years   spaces that cannot be so counted

not a conceptual exercise   this jumping   for this white i
jumping between among with lines dis\connections where i
have ignored spirits   tried to kill spirits   and from which
spirits have fled

you and she   she says   weave ropes from the dried leaves of
the iris   play jump rope with an iris string   by the trees
looking out at the ocean   friends pass the end of the braid to
her to you and continue jumping jumping   *by the trees*
looking out at the ocean   she says   friends pass an end of the green
plastic rope to her to me and continue jumping jumping

you and she chant   she says   while friends   eyes on the rope circling circling   feel the rope touching ground touching   choose the moment dart into the circling   skip through the circling   while you she turn the rope   a flying snake circling   friends jump fast so fast fast fast and faster   until a friend who just now does not jump quite quickly enough   pauses   catches her breath   takes in her hand your end of the rope and turns it

i and she chant   she says   while friends   eyes on the rope circling circling   feel the rope touching ground touching choose the moment   dart into the circling   skip through the circling while you   i   turn the rope   circling   friends jump high blur high higher   blurring into sky ocean earth friends until a friend who just now does not jump quite quickly enough pauses   catches her breath   takes in her hand my end of the rope and turns it

tales which i speak   tales which are told to me   tales which
edge undermine affect my own   *no tale   she says   is merely
yours merely mine   the edging undermining affecting is so complete*
there are also   she says   tales which can never be mine
which can never be yours

you're here already this morning?   i hear you arrive   the sun
has set has risen where you live   you say   you you i walk
pink sunlight sand   dip toes in the still cold waves

in excess of theory   *jelly fish*   perhaps not entirely in excess of
writing   *s p i r i t s*   *blue waves*   *how do i i lunar rose you i she
love?*

she dives across the page dives under the waves   she flies a
kite with red orange streamers and lies on the sand with her
friend

she

bicycles

along

the

edges

of

the

she
slips over   pages
the top
of
the
hill

she?   which she?

YELLOW?   BLUE   YELLOW   YELLOW
    YELLOW   BLUE

breathing   voices of water and night   *breathing*
water   *breathing*   waternight   *breathing*
night

reverberations
moonflowers   estrellas fugaces
reverberaciones
flores lunares   falling stars

r e v e r b e r a t i o n s   moonflowers   estrellas fugaces
falling stars   flores lunares   r e v e r b e r a c i o n e s

moonflowers   r e v e r b e r a t i o n s
lunas fugaces   falling   moons en las estrellitas de flores
in starflowers   r e v e r b e r a c i o n e s

r e v e r b e r a c i o n e s   flores lunares   falling stars
estrellas fugaces   moonfloweres   r e v e r b e r a t i o n s

flores lunares   r e v e r b e r a c i o n e s
falling moons   cayendo   lunas in starflowers   en las
estrellitas de flores   r e v e r b e r a t i o n s

you say that you like it   the california coast   where this
afternoon yellow sunflowers and seagulls glide in the bright
blue sky   and that you are hot   sweating

we kiss laugh take off our shirts   we look kiss and laugh
again   while we whiz down highway 🛡

tu dices que te gusta   la costa de california   donde esta
tarde girasoles amarillos y gaviotas planean en el cielo azul
subido y que tienes calor   que estás sudando

nosotras nos besamos reímos nos quitamos las camisas
nosotras miramos nos besamos y reímos otra vez   mientras
que silbamos por la carretera 🐱

who's there?
   don't lose touch with the little shining one

   moving rocks

¿quién es?

no pierdas contacto con la pequeña que brilla

rocas que se mueven

en la bahía de Itacuruçá   tu me dices   aquí si nosotras
tenemos ganas de hacer algo   lo hacemos   sin esperar

y tu yo nos zambullimos   todas vestidas   en el mar tropical
a medianoche   brisas calurosas   nuestros vestidos se
secan mientras caminamos al pueblo

at the bay of Itacuruçá   you tell me   here if we want to do
something   we do it   without waiting

and you i plunge   all of our clothes on   into the tropical sea
caballitos de mar   at midnight   *seahorses*   warm breezes
mermaids   sirenas   our clothes dry as we walk to town

delta aquarides   pléiades

stars fall   a shower of stars   fly   scatter flicker   se
estrellan con otras estrellas   fly west   fly east until
morning   stars fly   cross each other   estrellas filantes a
shower of stars   one star and another star   thousands of
stars

delta aquarides   pleiades

estrellas caen   una lluvia de estrellas   vuelan   se esparcen
parpadean   clash with other stars   vuelan al oeste
vuelan al este hasta la madrugada   estrellas vuelan   se
cruzan unas a otras   falling stars una lluvia de estrellas
una estrella y otra estrella   miles de estrellas

¿cómo florecen las flores lunares que tocan floreos y dicen
flores?   ¿a flourish a flirtation   moonflowers   how does
each bloom?

¿cómo florecen *las flores lunares   a flourish a flirtation*   que
tocan floreos y dicen flores   *moonflowers   how does each
bloom?*

these *moonflowers*   round *sounds*   each *blooms*   estas *flores*
lunares   sonidos *redondos*   cada una *florece*

while two dance two dances simultaneously

mientras que dos bailan dos bailes simultáneamente

while three sing three songs

mientras que tres cantan tres canciones

2 x 2 ritmos   o   4 4 2 6 0 3 9   2   9   6   ritmos   3 x 3
 rhythms or   4 3 1 4 6 7   2   1   1   6   5 ∞   rhythms
more or less   más o menos

2 x 2 rhythms   or   4 4 2 6 0 3 9   2   9   6   rhythms
 3 x 3   ritmos   o   4 3 1 4 6 7   2   1   1   6   5 ∞   ritmos
más o menos   more or less

y las memorias   nubes de mar y roca   tocan como agujeros
en el tiempo

_____

and memories   clouds of sea and rock   touch like holes in
time

———————————

tu agarras el juego de campanas   maritza   mari   mar
región helada cuando yo   apilando leña   te vi   con un
you who startled me in this icy region when i   stacking
walking over the snow-covered fields

maritza   tu que amas tanto la mar   you who love the ocean so
each other   tu que me dijiste   you who told me   que no
español that you do not speak english and that no one at the
fines de la primavera   tu lo hablas un poco   although now

marinera   *you hold the chimes*   tu que me asustaste en esta
bebé atado a tu espalda   andando sobre el campo nevado
firewood   saw you   with a baby tied to your back

much   tu yo nos asustábamos la una a la otra   you i startled
hablas el inglés y que nadie en la casa donde vives habla el
house where you live speaks spanish   aunque ahorita a
in late spring   you speak english some

tu agarras el juego de campanas   maritza   mientras que sobre
floating bridge   tu   mas alta que yo   levantas el brazo a los
colgar las campanas   y tu yo la anudamos   you   taller
cord to hang the chimes   and you i knot it

sobre el puente flotante   metal   madera   viento   el juego de
bridge   metal   wood   wind   the chimes in the spring rain

el puente flotante   you hold the chimes   maritza   while on the
árboles   lanzas alrededor de una rama una cuerda para
than me   reach up into the trees   toss around a branch a

campanas en la lluvia de primavera repica   *on the floating*
ring

ondas alfa amplificadas   despiertan despertadas por una
amplified alpha waves   awaken awakened by an abundance
viva   spring tide   marejada   undercurrent   ondulaciones
oceanic undulations distant gales seismic disturbances
growth

marejadas de sonido   soundswells   rodeadas por un grupo
surrounded by an endless group of large and small bells that

abundancia de silenciosreverberantessonidosreverberantes
of reverberantsilencesreverberantsounds   *maritza   marea*
oceánicas ventarrones distantes tumultos sismológicos
crecimiento rápido y espontáneo   rapid and spontaneous

sin fin de campanas y campanitas que empiezan a sonar
begin to sound

y una noche hay ojos en el juego de campanas   ojos que
centellean   ojos de una serpiente   amiga de una campesina
ojos que cuelgan del árbol sobre este puente flotante de
sueños

and one night there are eyes in the chimes   eyes that glisten
eyes of a snake   a farmer's friend   *¿había ojos?   sí   sí había
ojos*   eyes that hang from the tree over this floating bridge
of dreams

sonic readings   sonic writings   sonic events   where 1 is 2 or 3
or 7 and each is also one   disturbances embellishments
surprises confusions   an attentiveness an unusual
excitement modifications of

flores lunares   una escritura primaveral   de noche
iridiscente bajo las anchas hojas de los lirios   y que se abren
ruidosamente acá y allá en el monte

lecturas sónicas   escrituras sónicas   acontecimientos
sónicos   donde 1 es 2 o 3 o 7 y cada es también una
disturbios embellecimientos sorpresas confusiones   una
atención una excitación ínsolita modificaciones de

moonflowers   a spring writing   at night iridescent under
the broad leaves of lilies   and that open noisely here and
there in the woodlands

tu yo nosotras   conversaciones improvisaciones   eslabones
disyuntivos   dos voces o más y ninguna provee El Eslabón
ni obligadas ni ensartadas juntas ni adelante ni detrás   a la
deriva

oceans of worlds   lavender lightning bolts   guitars voices
feathers   multiple tunings   eddies of silences and sounds

you i we   conversations improvisations   disjunctive
linkings   two or more voices and none supplies The Link
not obliged not skewered together not ahead or behind
adrift

océanos de mundos   relámpagos lavanda   guitarras voces
plumas   entonaciones múltiples   remolinos de silencios y
sonidos

garlands of roses   whirling mirrors   zebras giraffes horses
gallop prance amble   music in green yellow red sounds
and the riders on the zebras   giraffes   lions   horses   cry
out too in green yellow orange red sounds   a merry-go-
round on the edge of this beach   whirling mirrors
garlands of roses

puentes flotantes   ¿de dónde? ¿a dónde?   conocido y
desconocido   transiciones mágicas e inesperadas   por eso
se dice que flotan

guirnaldas de rosas   espejos arremolinandos   cebras
avestruces jirafas   caballos   galopan hacen cabriolas
amblan   música en sonidos verdes amarillos naranjas rojos
y los jinetes sobre las cebras   avestruces   jirafas   leones
caballos   gritan también en sonidos verdes amarillos
naranjas rojos   una tiaviva al borde de esta playa   espejos
arremolinandos   guirnaldas de rosas y violetas y orquídeas
y azahares

floating bridges   from where? to where?   known and
unknown   magical and unexpected transitions   this is why
one says that they float

un softball   una frisbee mandarina   un paso rápido
   tu tiras el softball alto tan alto en el aire   y tu yo nosotras
nos acercamos   miramos hacia arriba   tu saltas alto
saltas altísimo tras el softball   y cojes un pedazo de cielo
           a través alrededor más allá de cada una   tu yo
nosotras tiramos cojemos tiramos la frisbee mandarina   7
veces 8 veces 9 veces   hasta que una tira de la frisbee
mandarina que va lejos   muy lejos

                                        tu vuelves
corriendo con la frisbee mandarina   justo a tiempo para ver
el softball cayendo   por las nubes cayendo del cielo   *el disco*
verde lima que gira en el otro juego   mientras que tu tiras yo
cojo tu tu yo tiramos y cojemos la frisbee mandarina   una
tirada lejos   yo corro y corro tras el softball   casi cojo el
softball   que se escurre de entre las manos y se cae en la mar

a lime green spinning disc   a beachball in six bright colors   the
beachball slips through your hands   bounces   rolls on the sand as
you i we run after it   you almost catch up with   you fall   when
   the beachball in six bright colors lifts you over the lime green
spinning disc   lifts you up up and away   your long hair flying

       & a tangerine frisbee lands in the midst of the game
tu corres   *you say you are tired and run off to play with your*
a lo largo   *friend   you i we come close then far as we throw*
del juego   tu te   *catch throw the spinning disc   4 times 8 times*
entras en el juego y recojes rápidamente la frisbee mandarina
12 times   until the lime green spinning disc   a long throw   gets
lost in the ♩ ♪ ♩ ♩ ♪ ♪ *passing by   two of whom toss*

un disco verde lima que gira   una pelota de playa en seis colores
brillantes   la pelota de playa se escurre de entre tus manos
rebota   rueda en la arena   mientras que tu yo nosotras corremos
detras de ella   tu casi la alcanzas   tu te caes   cuando la pelota
de playa en seis colores brillantes te eleva sobre el disco verde lima
que gira   te eleva alto más alto y a lo lejos   tu cabello largo
volando

       & una frisbee mandarina aterriza en medio del juego

tu dices que estás fatigada y te vas a jugar con tu   you run
amiga   tu yo nosotras nos acercamos entonces   along the edge
nos alejamos   mientras que tiramos cojemos tiramos   of the game
el disco verde que gira   4 veces 8 veces 12 veces   you slip into
hasta que el disco   the game and scoop up the tangerine frisbee
verde lima que gira   una tirada larga   se pierde en las ⚥ ⚥ ⚥ ⚥
⚥ ⚥ *que pasan   dos de las cuales tiran*

a softball   a tangerine frisbee   a fast pass   you throw
the softball high so high in the air   and you i we gather
round   look up   you leap high   leap very high after the
softball   and catch a piece of sky   through
around past each other   you i we throw catch throw the
tangerine frisbee   7 times 8 times 9 times   until a throw of
the tangerine frisbee that goes far   very far

you come back running with the tangerine frisbee   just in
time to see the softball falling   through the clouds falling
out of the sky   *the lime green spinning disc into the other game*
    while you throw i catch you you i throw and catch the
tangerine frisbee   a throw far off   i run and run after the
softball   almost catch the softball   which slips through my
hands and falls into the sea

anxiety of the literal would turn oceans of worlds into The
Familiar and The Foreign   literal: to the letter of   whose
law?   why a law?   floating bridges break off at the line |
  INS Immigration and Naturalization Service
    which would assign here what it counts as natural and
    here what it deems not to serve its law
not admitted   deported   admit only if correct documents
are in hand

planeando contra alrededor de cada una   todo rebota acá y allá sin
around *each other   everything bounces here and there without*

ansiedad de lo literal convertiría océanos de mundos en Lo
Familiar y Lo Ajeno   literal: según la letra de   ¿la ley de
quién?   ¿porqué una ley?   puentes flotantes se rompen en
la linea?
la migra   INS   Immigration and Naturalization Service
    que asignaría aquí lo que vale como natural y
    aquí lo que juzga no servir su ley
no se admiten   deportadas   admite sólo si tiene los
documentos correctos en mano

preocuparse de perdida o de ganancia   gliding against
concern for loss or gain

a wild goose chase   to chase a wild goose   and if that bird
cannot be caught   the will to catch another   to have the
wild in hand   to have Meaning in hand   such a reader
wears camouflage   not for the wild geese   but for herself

circundando zambulliendo planeando   los grillos al lado del

una caza de grillos   cazar unos grillos   y si un grillo no se
puede cojer   la voluntad de cojer otro   tener lo silvestre en
mano   tener El Sentido en mano   una tal lectora se silencia
a sí misma llevando camuflaje   no para los grillos   *si son
grillos*   sino para sí misma

arroyo salen volando   circling plunging soaring   the wild
geese by the stream fly off

marejadas de sonido   soundswells

to let vibrate until the sounds and silences fade away dejar

———————————

vibrar hasta que los sonidos y silencios se apaguen

———————————

cara   cabeza de atrás   *digo* _____   cara ojos abiertos
cara ojos cerrados   un espacio oscuro   cara dos ojos
abiertos   un espacio oscuro   cara dos ojos cerrados   un
espacio en blanco   cara   tres ojos cerrados   cabeza de
atrás   *tu dices* _____ *son la vista la más bella sobre
esta tierra aún verde*   cabeza de atrás   luz brillante   cara
ojos abiertos   tres ojos medio abiertos   espacio oscuro
pero tu dices   que cualquiera que uno ama es

face   back of head   *i say* _____   face eyes open   face
eyes closed   a dark space   face two eyes open   a dark
space   face two eyes closed   a blank space   face   three
eyes closed   back of head   *you say* _____ *are the*
most beautiful sight on this still green earth   back of head
bright light   face eyes open   three eyes half open   dark
space   *but you say   that whatever one loves is*

¿vosotras queréis estar todas en la misma página?   ¿algo
sobre lo que podáis escribir?   *¿tu?   ¿tu prefieres no escribir?*
tu y yo hablando desde ayer por la tarde

adoro los planetas   me dices   quiero ser astrónoma   tu
preguntas   ¿has vivido un gran amor?

you all want to be on the same page?   something to write
on?   *and you?   you prefer not to write?   you and i talking since*
yesterday afternoon

i adore the planets   you tell me   i want to be an astronomer
    you ask   have you lived a great love?

es una vía larga para nosotras   alcanzando de la tierra
para hallar   entre todas las cosas   ésta página

nuestros senderos se cruzaban cuando nosotras   buscando
las partes perdidas de nuestros cuerpos   nos cruzábamos
y después nos encontrábamos de nuevo en las celebraciones
    x recobró recientemente las partes perdidas de su cuerpo
del - --- - - -----

cada una de nosotras se turna ayundando a cada mujer que
llega aquí encontrar todo de sí misma que ella desea recoger
    para algunas es su cuerpo   para algunas es una
conexión   para algunas son sus espíritus   para algunas

a veces una parte se encuentra en lugares que nosotras no
te describiremos   a veces una mujer se desliza en un
bosillo de su imaginación y está a salvo mientras que es
    asesinada   tratamos de estar con una mujer si ella
quiere que estemos allá

somos tantas aquí   aunque no tenemos nuestros cuerpos
terrestres   hay muchos poderes de las que hacemos uso

                    tus hermanas de la mar

it is a long way for us   reaching back to earth to find
  among all things   this page

our paths crossed when we   looking for the missing parts
of our bodies   passed by each other   and later we met
again at the celebrations   x recently retrieved the lost
parts of her body from the - - -   - - - - - -

each of us takes turns helping each womon who arrives
here locate all of herself that she wants to gather up   for
some it is her body   for some it is a connection   for some
it is her spirits   for some

at times a part is found in places that we will not describe
    at times a womon slips into a pocket of her imagination
and is safe while being murdered   we try to be with a
womon if she wants us to be there

we are so many here   although we do not have our
terrestrial bodies   there are many powers of which we
make use

                              your sisters of the sea

hoy tu y yo caminamos alrededor de la ilha grande   *te digo*
que escribo y enseño   quiero ser astrónoma   tu me dices   pero
no podía continuar con la escuela   despues de limpiar oficinas por
la noche y en el día   tu y yo subimos las calles colinosas a la
playa donde comemos hamburguesas y ananá fresco y
sacamos fotos con tu máquina

whitewimmin brownwimmin blackwimmin passing near lives of
this whitewommon passing near   mujeresblancas
mujeresmorenas mujeresnegras pasando cerca unas vidas de
otras mujeresnegras mujeresrojas mujeresamarillas
mujeresmorenas mujeresblancas   durante dos semanas o
tiempos indefinidos

today you and i walk around ilha grande   i tell you that i write
and teach   i want to be an astronomer   you tell me   but i
could not continue with school   after cleaning offices at
night and in the day   *you and i climb the hilly streets to the*
beach where we eat hamburgers and fresh pineapple and take
photos with your camera

mujeresblancas mujeresmorenas mujeresnegras pasando
cerca unas vidas de esta mujerblanca pasando cerca
   whitewimmin brownwimmin blackwimmin passing near lives of
other blackwimmin redwimmin yellowwimmin brownwimmin
whitewimmin   during two weeks or indefinite times

language almost familiar and not quite familiar   te entiendo
pero el ritmo   el ritmo as distinto   i've always spoken
english   but   sí hablo el español   pero tu castellano me
cuesta algo

una gimnástica acústica   an acoustic gymnastics   inquieta   *de*
torcidas   dentro de   entre   en medio de   uneasy   *within*
i you we

lengua casi familiar y no muy familiar   *i understand you*
but the rhythm   the rhythm is distinct   siempre hablé el inglés
pero   yes i speak spanish   but your castilian takes me some work

lenguas y memorias   *ásperas*   of languages and memories
between   among   grating   *cada yo tu nosotras*   strained   *each*

translations   crossings   *aquí todo está traducido   casi*
  NOT TO CARRY ACROSS BY FORCE   TO RESIST A
FORCED CROSSING

and where there are crossings   *irregular   non-sequential   non-interchangeable*   perhaps there are only crossings   *tones delay cluster drone*

traducciones travesías   *here everything is translated   almost*
  RESISTIR UNA TRAVESIA FORZADA   NO LLEVAR AL
TRAVÉS A LA FUERZA

y donde hay travesías   *irregulares   no-secuenciales   no-*
intercambiables   quizás hay solamente travesías   *tonos demoran*
se arraciman   zumban

cultural linguistic dissolves   intonations at once distinct fluid
blurred   where by force or choice or habit   the shores fade
away   or appear for just a moment   or have vanished   or
never were

these slow unfoldings of hearts   myriad spacestimes between
that fly and collide   in which we we you i neither stay nor leave
unchanged

— — — — — —

disoluciones lingüísticas culturales   entonaciones a la vez
distintas fluídas empañadas   donde por fuerza o por
elección o por hábito   las orillas se desdibujan   o aparecen
apenas un momento   o se han desvanecido   o nunca fueron

estos despliegues lentos de corazones   espaciostiempos
miríadas entre   que vuelan y se chocan   en los cuales
nosotras nosotras tu yo ni nos quedamos ni partimos
incambiadas

— — — — — — —

you and i   along the streets of this port town   a
neighborhood appears   i learned the man's part so i could
do the tango with my dyke friends   but none of my dyke
friends knows the tango   maría you say

tango   tocar tambor   truenos y relampagos de shango
  bailar ni mirando directamente ni mirando lejos de

tu y yo   a lo largo de las calles de ésta ciudad porteña   un
barrio aparece   aprendí la parte del hombre para poder
bailar el tango con mis amigas tortilleras   pero ninguna de
mis amigas tortilleras conoce el tango   dices tu maría

tango   to play a tambor   thunderclaps and lightning of
shango   to dance neither looking directly at nor looking
away from

arms   hands   yemas de dedo   legs   climbing up   *feet*
circling down   around one branch up over and around
another   *i   you   who?   which who?   is there a who?*
silvia claudia maría cristina leonor jef   *hear she and she on
the grass below running hand in hand*

el ombu   una hierba   no un árbol   más grande que
muchísimos arboles   sombra en los cielos abiertos de las
pampas   tronco inmenso de hierba esponjosa   ni madera
 corteza de pellejo de elefante

brazos   manos   fingertips   piernas   subiendo arriba   *pies*
circundando hacia abajo   alrededor de una rama por encima
y alrededor de otra   *¿yo   tu   quién?   ¿cuál quién?   ¿hay*
un quién?   *silvia sarah claudia gabriella gloria maría cristina*
leonor jef   aroma de un banquete biftec palmitos y   oímos
ella y ella sobre la hierba abajo corriendo mano en mano

the ombu   an herb   not a tree   larger than many a tree
shade in the open skies of the pampas   immense trunk of
spongey herb   not wood   bark of elphant skin

        he pasado una de mis vidas pintando el ombu
        en las estaciones cambiantes   sigo pintando
        mercedes tu me dices   i have passed one of
        my lives painting the ombu in changing
        seasons   i keep on painting   mercedes you
        tell me

treading water   i hear you on the beach dancing   *milonga*
  sandía you and she   *merengue*   dancing   *catimbo   reggae
eléctrico*   beside the palm trees   she and she

bailando   *bahiaos*   al lado de las palmas   *lambada*
bailando y
                              mientras que jef yo nado   brazada
de mariposa   crol   rana   crol de espalda   alrededor de las
islas
sunrise tellen de la salida del sol   *ghost* murex fantasma   *ala
de* angel wing

pedaleando en el egua   te oigo sobre la playa bailando
candomblé   sandía tu y ella   *pagode*   bailando   al lado de
las palmeras   ella y ella

dancing   *mambo*   by the palm trees   *rumba*   dancing and
                                        while jef i swim   butterfly
crawl   frog   backstroke   around the islands
zebra periwinkle cebra   *dove shell* columbella   concha
estrella starshell

i who mercedes has not yet painted   on summer evenings
jef i open the doors to the garden   a garden not unlike the
one where marjorie you were murdered   and each evening
a spider   web suspended from rooftop   to the orange tree
by the door   across the steps   and rosegarden   spins the
web it has eaten the night before

jef   ésa jef-ee.uu.-yo   ésa jef-ee.uu.-tu   configuraciones
conflictivas   ésas nancy van kitty gloría ana anne jef chris
¿-ee.uu.-yo   -ee.uu.-tu   -ee.uu.-nosotras?

yo a quien mercedes todavía no ha pintado   por las tardes
veraniegas   jef yo abro las puertas al jardín   un jardín no
desemejante a aquel donde marjorie tu fuiste asesinada   y
cada tarde una araña   tela suspendida del techo   al
naranjo al lado de la puerta   a traves de las gradas   y la
rosaleda   hila la tela que ha comido la noche anterior

jef   this jef-u.s.a.-i   this jef-u.s.a.-you   conflicted
configurations   these claudia sarah edwina maría   elise jo
maritza -u.s.a.-i   -u.s.a.-you   -u.s.a.-we?

miro por la ventana al arroyo donde jef tu y yo   comienzos de
primavera   mapaches venados   contando cuentos escuchando
cuentos   de mi mamá y su alfarería en el campo   y de como
maritza yo no puedo regresar allá   de tus amigas tu hermana   de
como una de mis hermanas   atrapada en el tiroteo cruzado   fue
asesinada por la lucha en las calles de tegucigalpa
              del miedo que tengo a vivir en aquella ciudad
quiero quedar aquí más tiempo   solo un rato   cuidando a nicole
aunque cocino y limpio por ellos   nicole comienza a hablar
yendo a la iglesia   y entonces tal vez un curso de inglés o   - -
- - -   -   *mañana jef tu y yo tomaremos*
fotos

hemisferios   distinct and not entirely distince   racimos de
vidas   resistencia   nuclear power plants   celebraciones
BRUJAS   fronteras   minas a la deriva   capuchinas
amarillas rojas naranjas saltan por las laderas fragantes con
mimosa   wisteria

i look out the window to the stream where jef you and i   early
spring   raccoons deer   story telling story listening   of my
mother and her pottery-making in the countryside   and how
maritza i cannot return there   of your friends your sister   of how
one of my sisters   caught in the cross-fire   was killed by the
fighting in the streets of tegucigalpa
                        of the fear i have to live in that city   i want to stay
here longer   just awhile   taking care of nicole   although i cook
and clean for them   nicole is beginning to speak   going to
church   and then perhaps an english class or   - -
- -   -   tomorrow jef you and i will take
photos

hemispheres   distintos y no enteramente distintos   clusters
of lives   resistance   centrales nucleares   celebrations
WITCHES   boundary lines   drifting mines   nasturtiums
yellow red orange bound down hillsides fragrant with
mimosa   vistaria   jazmines   bouganvilla

querida maritza

¡hola!   te envio un abrazo fuerte   ¿cómo
estas?
cuando no viniste ayer por la mañana para
sacar fotos esperé y entonces fuí a tu casa   pero no
estuviste allá   no había nadie   no podía descifrarlo
estuve inquieta   ya que ellos nunca te llevan a
ninguna parte con ellos   hoy por la mañana cuando
fuí otra vez era demasiado tarde
pienso que insistieron que tomes el avión
inmediatemente y si tu rehusaste dijeron que te
denunciarían   ellos te arrastraron al aeropuerto
vaya nuestro trabajo para que esto no te pasara y por tu
empleo nuevo que hubiera comenzado pronto - - - - - -
-    -
gracias por el libro que me dejaste con la
dirección de tu hermana en tegucigalpa y tu nota
además

dear maritza

    hello!   i send you a big hug   how are you?
    when you did not come by yesterday morning
to take photos i waited and then i went over to your
house   but you weren't there   no one was there   i
couldn't figure it out   i was worried as they never
take you anywhere with them   this morning when i
went over again it was too late
    i gather they insisted that you fly back
immediately and if you refused they said they would
report you   they just took you off to the airport   so
much for our work to keep this from happening and for
your new job that would have begun soon   - - - - - -
    thanks so much for the book you left with your
sister's address in tegucigalpa and your note
besides

querida jef

-- - -- -- --   -   - - - - - - - -

yo aquí estoy bien con mi familia   vivo con mi
hermana   sólo que un poco triste pues no he
podido encontrar trabajo   pero todo me ha sido
difícil

                    que te encuentres buenita de salud

                         Maritza

dear jef

-- -   -- -- --   -   - - - - - - - -
i am alright here with my family   i'm living with
my sister   except i'm a little sad because i haven't
been able to find any work   but everything has been
difficult for me

hoping that you are well

Maritza

un arroyo garzas azules venados abedules de plata
caminando en el agua saltando de piedra en piedra buscando un
sentido para cruzar   tu nosotras tu yo nosotras   hacemos
pausa nos sentamos sobre una roca y dejamos caer
flojamente las piernas   hacemos pausa nos zambullimos
nadamos chapoteamos nos asoleamos   tu nosotras tu yo
nosotras nos tiramos saltamos al través   miramos no solo
agua o solo piedras o solo arroyo o solo las orillas del arroyo
   o arroyo y no cielo o árboles

- - - - - - -   - - -   - - - - - - - - - well as i told you i ended
up living with my sister here in the city   i'm rather
sad because i've already been here 4 months and still

a stream blue herons deer silver birches   *wading rockhopping looking for a way to cross*   you we you i we   pause sit on a rock and dangle legs   pause jump in swim splash sun   you we you i we tumble in leap across   watch not only water or only stones or only stream or only banks of stream   or stream and not sky or trees

- - - - - - -   - - -   - - - - - - - - - pues como te había dicho que me quedaría a vivir con mi hermana aquí en la cuidad

   estoy bastante triste porque ya tengo 4 meses de estar aquí y aún

rockhopping is not to fill a stream with stones   nor is
friendship to amass accurate information until one has IT
points in common are perhaps as uncertain as stones with
    moss   streams may rise or may dry up   stones may tilt
and turn

      no he podido encontrar trabajo   aurita está muy
      difícil aquí conseguir empleo bueno   lo demás está
      bien

      saludame a tus amigas   te saludo con mucho amor

                    maritza

———————————

saltando de piedra en piedra no es llenar un arroyo con
piedras   ni es una amistad amasar información hasta que
uno LO tiene   puntos comunes son quizás tan inciertos
    como piedras con musgo   arroyos pueden crecer o
pueden secarse completamente   piedras pueden ladearse y
darse vuelta

    i've not been able to find work   right now it is very
hard to get a good job here   but apart from that
everything is fine

    my regards to your friends
    yours with much love

    maritza

the california coast   where late this afternoon elise you jef i
splash saltwater over your my sunburned backs   you i
stretch out at high tide on a rock   waves swirling   seagulls
a bright blue sky

the page across   just over there   do you

la página a través   justo allá   ¿tu   yo   lo

la costa de california   donde a fines de esta tarde elise tu jef
yo chapoteamos agua salada sobre tus mis espaldas
quemadas del sol   tu yo nos tendemos cuando la marea está
alta sobre un escollo   ondas remolineando   gaviotas   un
cielo azul subido

do i   bypass it?   wander   collide   cross paths in
it? skip on through?
desviamos?   ¿vagamos   nos chocamos   nos
cruzamos los sentidos en ella?   ¿brincamos de un
lado al otro?

no fixed i on which to set one's sights   you you i i we   who
may or may not meet   according to astrological
correspondence   suns moons or?

a round drum a large drum a cylinder drum a brass drum a
small drum   tocadas simultaneamente por varias   tocan sin
parar   palos de agua   traza viento   chatarra   pedacitos
hallados

no yo fijo en el cual fijar la vista   tu tu yo yo nosotras
quienes podemos o no podemos encontrarnos   según una
correspondencia astrológica   ¿soles lunas o?

un tambor redondo un tambor grande un bombo una
zabumba un tamboril   played simultaneously by several
play on and on   water sticks   wind trace   metal scraps
found pieces

dear sandía

    the economic situation here gets worse and
worse   i do not know how long you i and brasilisa
can stay in this room   mailing now and then the
machine parts   to the amazon
    i know a womon   she went to the u.s. and
returned with enough money to buy herself a house
but would you or i or both of us go   and how?   you
almost 30 years younger than me   mother and
daughter not exactly   though·you grew up with me
like brasilisa is growing up with you   found   a
chance encounter   or not so much chance   i
passing nearby the church steps   like you passing
nearby the pile of trash   -   -
    where at sunrise on these beaches cariocas
life grows sturdily and with dreams

               a kiss

               maría luisa

    una acrobacia de la lectura   ojos resbalan al través de
la espina encorvada   la espina flexible   que se mueve
hace juglarías   pasa las páginas   echa de un capirotazo las
páginas   se parte   a todas partes páginas y más páginas
y entre las páginas

querida sandía

    la situación económica aqui se hace peor y peor
no se cuanto tiempo tu yo y brasilisa   podemos
quedarnos en este cuarto   echando al correo de vez
en cuando las partes de las máquinas al amazonas
    conozco una mujer   ella se fue a los ee.uu. y
volvió con bastante dinero para comprarse una casa
    pero sería tu o yo o ambas de nosotras que iría?
tu   así 30 años más joven que yo madre e hija no
precisamente   bien que tu crecías conmigo como
brasilisa está creciendo contigo   hallada   un
encuentro por casualidad   o no tanto por casualidad
    yo pasando cerca de las gradas de la iglesia   como
tu pasando cerca del montón de basura   -   -
    donde a la salida del sol en estas playas
cariocas la vida crece fuerte y tenaz y con sueños

          un beso

         maría luisa

    an acrobatics of reading   eyes slide across   the spine
supple   the spine flexible   that moves   juggles   turns
pages   flips pages   splits   everywhere pages and more
pages   and between the pages

-- -- - - - -   bueno de aquí jef te puedo contar
que la situación económica está cada día peor   con
una inflación de 70% por mes las cosas suben de
precio todo los días y está siendo muy dificil seguir
viviendo aquí   ayer gané un poco cuando mandé a
manaus   a las minas allá   unas partes para las
máquinas

    sandía estaba trabajando en una joyería pero se
sofocó y a ella la operaron de emergencia

como charlamos aquí   mi deseo es ir allí   ¿ya sabes
a que   verdad?   te pido por favor veas para mi
algo si es possible

        cuéntame como estás   cuéntame algo de tí

            besitos y un abrazo   míos y de sandía

                    maría luisa

querida amiga

        te imagino ahora   maría luisa in your room
in front of the panoramic mural of the beach   white
sand islands mangos papayas palms   in the
background hills of río   just like the photo you sent

        how is sandía?   what were the two sheep eyes
by

-- -- ---- well from here jef i can tell you that
the economic situation gets worse every day   with
an inflation of 70% each month things cost more
everyday and it is becoming very difficult to continue
living here   yesterday i earned a little when i sent to
manaus   to the mines there   some machine parts

    sandía was working in a jewelry store but she
couldn't breathe and passed out and they did an
emergency operation on her

since we are chatting here   my desire is to go there
you already know for what   don't you?   i ask you
please see if there is something for me if you can

        tell me how you are   tell me something about
yourself

                    kisses and a hug from me and from sandía

                                    maría luisa

dear friend

        i imagine you now   maría luisa en tu cuarto
frente a la muralla panorámica de la playa   arena
blanca islas mangos papayas palmas   a la
lontananza las colinas de río   justo como la foto que
tu me mandaste

        ¿como está sandía?   ¿que hacían los dos ojos
de óveja al

lado de la puerta cuando ella se desmayó?   es que
ella   - - - -   - - - -   - - - -

   estoy ahorita en california   la escuela este año
me ha sido dificil   & veré lo que viene

he ido andando con amigas en las playas aquí y   - -
- - - - - - -   - - -   - - - - - - - - - - - - - - - -

                              cariños besitos

                                        jef

la costa de california   donde al final de esta tarde elise tu jef
yo   *jef tu   de quien sandía yo diría* - -   - - -   tu tu yo
nosotras y nosotras   who mercedes i have not painted
who mercedes you   across between the shimmering of
   deaths-lives   continue painting

the door doing when she passed out?   does she   - - - -
- - - -   - - - -

       i am now in california   school this year has
been difficult   & i'll see what is next

i've been walking with friends on the beaches here
and - -   - - - - - - -   - - -   - - - - - - - - - - - - - - - - -

                 cariños kisses

                   jef

the california coast   where late this afternoon elise you jef i
jef you   of whom sandía i would say - -   - -   - - -   you you
i   we and we   a quienes mercedes yo todavía no he pintado
a quienes mercedes tu   a través entre lo tornasolado de
  muertes-vidas   sigues pintando

a travelling music these moonflowers travelling   among
between   around   stars travelling   among   between
around blue eyes   brown eyes   green eyes   black eyes
hazel eyes   tourmaline eyes   cobalt eyes   aquamarine eyes
obsidian eyes travelling

*ellas vinieron del arroyo y se sentaron en la orilla   ellas vinieron
de las olas y se estiraron al lado de vos en la arena cerca de los
acantilados*

una música viajera esas flores lunares viajando   en medio
de   entre   alrededor de   estrellas viajando   en medio de
entre   alrededor de ojos azules   ojos morenos   ojos verdes
ojos negros   ojos castaños claros   ojos obsidianos viajando

*she and she came out of the streams and sat on the banks   she
and she came out of the waves and stretched out next to you on the
sand by the cliffs*

for she who would come alive after torture and murder

for all that would come alive over and over

por ellas que vendrían vivas despúes de la tortura y el asesinato

theresa hak kung cha

marjorie allen

los desaparecidos

por toda la que vendría viva una y otra vez

have you lived a great love?

¿has vivido un gran amor?

tea on the beach at midnight

sound of the thighbone flute that carries her from land to
land   sound that can avert hailstorms   sound of the
thighbone flute carved bone of she who has died violently
    sound that can shake crumble a mountain   sound that
carries her to and from

your leg   you i open your leg again   lift away gluteus
maximus gluteus medius periformis   move across gemellus
obturator internus quadratus femoris   lift away and move
across until   you i   femur in countless pieces   arranging
pieces   drop in a metal bar   pat bone nerves blood vessels
    around bar   close   leg closed   your leg closed lid on a
jewel box gold with mirrors and angels   jewel box wood
    with dried spring flowers   while she who listens   she
who has been listening   lets out a scream and tears for what
is

you i she her   intimate chattings   near across what still
is happening   unstable junctions of midnight and morning
not only feathers but string not only sea grass but rocks sand
a bouncing moon and two trees running   sweet cakes a
blanket a thermos of hot tea   a feeling of instability before
dawn

there are some lands of beautiful noise terrible noise
    around the bay sun sparkling   eucalyptus pines hills
brown with drought roll down to the ocean   sea lions
early afternoon   beginning of summer in california
driving south on highway ⬡

crash metal glass again crash   how to keep alive at the
edge of life?   yes all things are connected   but please not
now   and my friends?   crash metal glass again crash
my body   this body at the edge of life   thin thin as
cellophane   body of luminous colors and light   crash
metal glass again crash   glass   i spit out glass and blood
spitting out glass   more glass   and blood

not to discard persistent disturbance   to resist continuous
prunings that would mark the random as not functional and
breed it out   her she you i invoked by wayside markers
that obscure

tones shapes gestures textures   myriad streams through
which energies pass   touched by their power to move
molecules atoms   you i   arms shoulders hands thicker
denser now   reach into her navel and pull out a crocus

running downhill over soft pine needles slowly   not raw
fear which has blown away   which has passed   but a
vortex pushing driving red   that flies up and out over your
shoulder   that whirls away   and in the tall grasses
rhinestones   pink blue lilac   swirl loop flip over and come
down   light rains of early spring

sonic shadows   echoes in a valley as unfinished
conversations touch   interferences inconveniences in each
sound produced where sound image event vary by
movement of the wind   if you i make time so that
shadows are heard   taking six different names in a lifetime
   two names for today when i am with you

tide going out   i skip from rock to rock   two eyes in the
rocks   i put my fingers through the two eyes and up comes
eyes wide and long across   mouth open   grey stone
checkbones cheeks chin   holes through mouth and left eye
   shells embedded in neck   unmistakably a face or not a
face at all

lost the car keys twice in two days   keys to engine and keys
to gas tank   out of gas and can't unlock the gas cap to add
more   you tell me on the phone that you wanted to make
a change   a change of direction   and are going west to the
green growing things

a sea of microtones   ambiguous tones of differing intervals
and unexpected effects   that color the hearts of you i she her
   that vary according to time of day season mood

life arising here and going away there   gathering dispersing
ageing emerging   according to environment and relations
among beings   microtonal spins

response improvisations   microtonal readings   combine
and recombine landscapes   drift along across nearby on the
edges of

the mouth as point of particularity and individuality   the
mouth dissolves

a tree on the beach   a tree of mouths   eyes at the peak of
upper lips   golden flashing eyes   hollow eyes at juncture
of lower and upper lips   a pink mouth   a peach mouth   a
buff mouth   brown mouths   red pink red purple mouths
green glowing mouths   salmon mouths

a page of mouths   a book of mouths   you i she her
vibrating intervals   neither fused nor entirely distinct
     mouths labial fleshy folds muscles   mouths labile   open
to change adaptable   undergoing chemical alteration
unstable   forgetful   wandering   liable to slip   mouths
slipping across deaths lives

an afterbirth with blood clots the size of tennis balls   color
of the brown pot over there   and pieces of the cosmic eggs
minutes before rolling by you i her in trance   dream
incubation   tonight visiting lands where   a loosening of
jaws   pouring rose water over jaws   whiskers   metal
whiskers   growing around jaws   whiskers long and so
heavy   then drop off   melt into the ground   metal and
spitting out glass   metal and glass over heart   pouring rose
water over jaws   as the debris comes out   look about
   there is so much of it

turning cartwheels   two bodies make one body   or three or
four bodies   arms legs flying   long shadows on the beach
how to do again what has been done   what is done   but
with a love   a ritual of healing?

absolute dividing line   before and after   forever lost and
never to be   two halves that cannot be pasted together
pushed together fused

how to love where there may be nothing in common?   this
today and (not) that tomorrow   as the line gallops plunges
   prances bucks   scatters   over distance   scenes
disentangling tangling   simultaneously cyclically
youyoush eiiheri iher sheyo ui   green star turquoise red
small pencil floats out of leg   intervals in diffusion
confusion   hammer chisel sit pause

so glad you called   yes she was to have
graduated from high school this year   summer had
arrived after a long winter and snow into the spring
driving with her two friends to a picnic at the inlet
the meadow had just turned green and the
woodlands were dotted with purple irises   and then
it happened   noontime   at the intersection by your
house   where the dirt roads cross next to the train
tracks

if only i could take her
place   she was my only daughter   if only it might
have been me instead

her best friend was taken to the hospital and
that night was found wandering around the morgue
looking for her

near the end of june   just one day after i had
arrived here in california
he was driving drunk at full speed in the wrong
direction on highway 🐱

you said that you wanted to get back your body   to
get back your life
i'm feeling lots better now   i spend most of
my time stretching strengthening doing physical
therapy pilates cybex nautilus   i hope to walk
again

of course i'll be glad to look after your house while
you're away   thanks   i'll be thinking of you

it is rumored that folk in the fairy-world have power to
charm the souls of such as are inclined to them forth from
their bodies in sleep and take them ajourneying in strange
lands

> ella young, "book of opal," *triptych*

scent of pink beach roses or   tall green reeds by the stream
she and she   hands in the water   hands huge ovals full of
    water   pass to you and you on the bank a small round
shape with a sun on it   a sun rising

the sunrise makes my shirt a little brighter
won't you come with me?   this field is dark and
chill   our breath is white   she carries her dead
    one dear one on her back   blossoming
    knowledge   earth roaring sound

connective tissues muscles webbing   once flexible elastic
resiliant   now intervals bunched together undifferentiated
glued

looking at the leg   touching the leg   hands on left leg right
   leg rub one hour daily for four months   notice where
kneecap is stuck and adjust hand pressure accordingly   and
your leg my leg may bend   tissues memories lift separate
slowly release spin out

some say that she and her could light fires by singing certain
songs   or bring rain   melt stones   cause flowers to bloom
draw birds and animals around a peaceful circle of singing
musicians

in compassionate celebration   happiness   my sorrow is
sorrow you are nearby my happiness   how to say your
   sorrow is my sorrow your happiness is my happiness?

you i she her   sound of mountains colliding   ocean sound
sound of the thighbone flute   and then   a moment later
they were gone